OUR
GRE★T
STATES

WHAT'S GREAT ABOUT
MISSOURI?

✳ Robin Koontz

LERNER PUBLICATIONS ✳ MINNEAPOLIS

CONTENTS

Copyright © 2016
by Lerner Publishing Group, Inc.

Content Consultant: Jon E. Taylor, PhD
Associate Professor of History
University of Central Missouri

Lerner Publications Company
A division of Lerner Publishing Group, Inc.
241 First Avenue North
Minneapolis, MN 55401 USA

For reading levels and more information, look up this title at www.lernerbooks.com.

Main body text set in ITC Franklin Gothic Std Book Condensed 12/15.
Typeface provided by Adobe Systems.

Library of Congress Cataloging-in-Publication Data

Koontz, Robin Michal.
    What's great about Missouri? / by Robin Koontz.
        pages cm. — (Our great states)
    Includes index.
    Audience: Grades 4–6.
    ISBN 978-1-4677-3883-5 (lb : alk. paper) — ISBN 978-1-4677-8509-9 (pb : alk. paper) — ISBN 978-1-4677-8510-5 (eb pdf)
    1. Missouri—Juvenile literature. I. Title.
F466.3.K66 2015
977.8—dc23   2015001954

Manufactured in the United States of America
1 – PC – 7/15/15

MISSOURI Welcomes You!

Let's explore Missouri! The Show-Me State is filled with fun outdoor activities. Enjoy a riverboat ride, hike trails, or explore caves. Or swim, fish, and boat at the Lake of the Ozarks. You can also visit one of the state's many museums and monuments. Learn more about science and history at the George Washington Carver National Monument. Or find your favorite celebrity at the Hollywood Wax Museum. This great state has much to offer! Keep reading to learn about ten amazing things that make Missouri fun to visit!

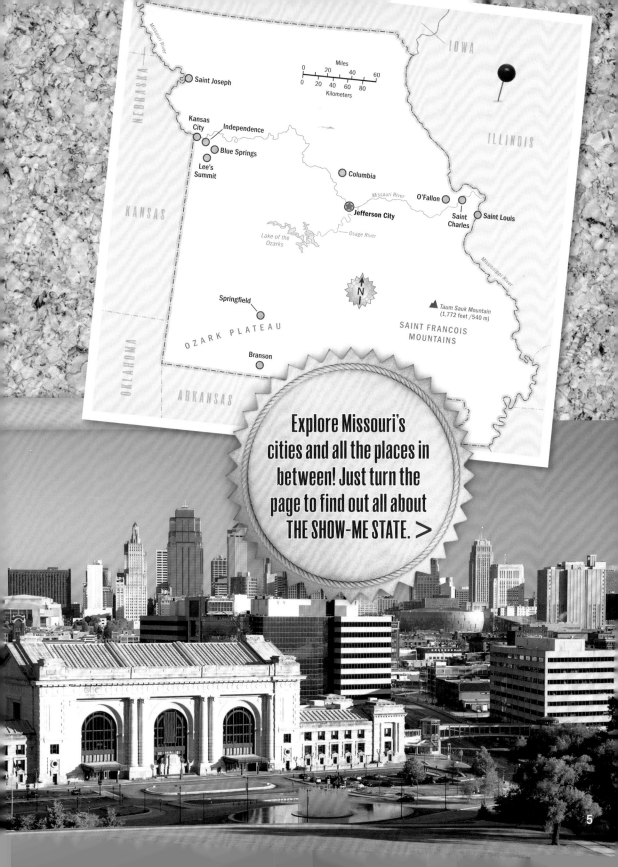

Miles
0 20 40 60

Kilometers
0 20 40 60 80

NEBRASKA

Missouri River

IOWA

ILLINOIS

Saint Joseph

Kansas City

Independence

Blue Springs

Lee's Summit

KANSAS

Columbia

Missouri River

O'Fallon

Saint Charles

Saint Louis

Jefferson City

Osage River

Lake of the Ozarks

Mississippi River

N

Springfield

Taum Sauk Mountain
(1,772 feet /540 m)

OZARK PLATEAU

SAINT FRANCOIS MOUNTAINS

OKLAHOMA

Branson

ARKANSAS

Explore Missouri's cities and all the places in between! Just turn the page to find out all about THE SHOW-ME STATE. >

GATEWAY ARCH

> Begin your visit to Saint Louis at one of the city's most famous spots—the Gateway Arch. It is the tallest monument in the United States. The arch is 630 feet (192 meters) high. You can travel to the top on a small tram. From the top, look through the windows at the city of Saint Louis below.

The arch is also called the Gateway to the West. This is because many traders and explorers moved through Saint Louis in the 1800s. They were traveling west to find and settle more land. Two of the most famous explorers to travel through Saint Louis were Meriwether Lewis and William Clark. Lewis and Clark visited many parts of the western United States. During their travels, the pair studied plants and animals, drew maps, and visited several American Indian nations.

After your visit to the arch, hop aboard a riverboat tour nearby. In the 1800s and the early 1900s, people used riverboats to travel up and down the Mississippi River.

MISSOURI RIVER

The Missouri River is the longest river in North America. It begins in the Rocky Mountains in western Montana. The river flows east and then south before connecting to the Mississippi River approximately 15 miles (24 kilometers) north of the Gateway Arch. The Missouri River flows through seven states including Montana, North Dakota, South Dakota, Nebraska, Iowa, Kansas, and Missouri.

On a clear day, you'll see the Mississippi River and miles of the Saint Louis landscape from the top of the Gateway Arch.

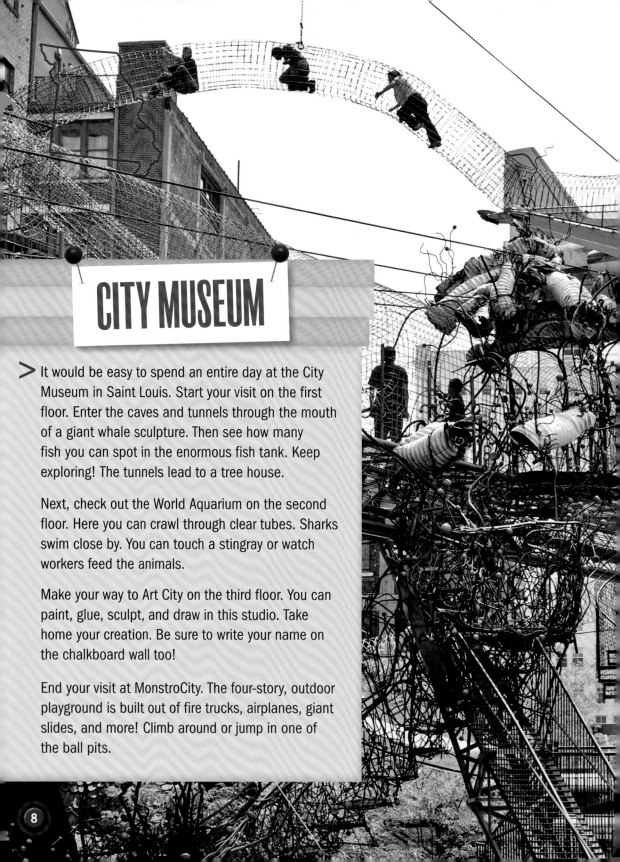

CITY MUSEUM

> It would be easy to spend an entire day at the City Museum in Saint Louis. Start your visit on the first floor. Enter the caves and tunnels through the mouth of a giant whale sculpture. Then see how many fish you can spot in the enormous fish tank. Keep exploring! The tunnels lead to a tree house.

Next, check out the World Aquarium on the second floor. Here you can crawl through clear tubes. Sharks swim close by. You can touch a stingray or watch workers feed the animals.

Make your way to Art City on the third floor. You can paint, glue, sculpt, and draw in this studio. Take home your creation. Be sure to write your name on the chalkboard wall too!

End your visit at MonstroCity. The four-story, outdoor playground is built out of fire trucks, airplanes, giant slides, and more! Climb around or jump in one of the ball pits.

What will you create in Art City?

Explore the inside of the giant whale on the first floor of the City Museum.

THE MAGIC HOUSE

Polygon Puzzle

Test your geometry skills at the Magic House's Math Path exhibit.

> Make your way to the Magic House in Saint Louis. This huge mansion became a children's museum in 1979. Over the years, the museum has expanded. These days, it is filled with tons of hands-on activities. Visitors can play, explore, create, and even solve mysteries here!

In the Children's Village, you can sell groceries, fix a car, or serve pizza. You can also catch a fish and climb a ladder to a tree house. After visiting the village, make your way to the Bubble Room. Blow a giant bubble and pop it. Or stand still as a giant bubble surrounds you! Head to the Art Studio to paint, color, and make other creations.

Become a detective in the Can You Solve the Mystery? exhibit. Find secret rooms and look at fingerprints and other clues. Then find out what it's like to be the president in the Star-Spangled Center. Give a speech, pretend to vote, and sing patriotic songs.

St. Louis Children's M

Would you like to give an animal a checkup at the pet clinic in the Children's Village?

cHouse

seum • 516 South Kirkwood Road

WILSON'S CREEK

> Wilson's Creek National Battlefield is just outside of Springfield. It is where the first Civil War (1861–1865) battle west of the Mississippi River occurred. Drive with your family along the 4.9-mile (7.9 km) road inside the park. There are eight stops along the way. You'll see homes, cabins, and spots where fighting happened during the battle.

Take a walking trail to go deeper into the park. Hike or ride on horseback through the park's 7 miles (11 km) of trails. You can also come to the park at night once a year for the annual candlelight tour. This special tour remembers people who were wounded or killed in battle.

Next, visit the Ray House inside the park. John Ray was a postmaster in Wilson's Creek. During the battle, Ray allowed soldiers to use his home as a hospital. If you're visiting in the summer months, you'll see reenactments of life during the Civil War at the park. Actors dress up in period clothing. They show you how weapons and medicine were used during the war.

GENERAL NATHANIEL LYON

The Battle of Wilson's Creek happened in August 1861. During the battle, Union general Nathaniel Lyon was hurt. People took him to John Ray's house to be treated. But no one could save him. He died because of his injuries. It was the first death of a Union general during the Civil War.

See the inside of a Civil War–era home at Wilson's Creek National Battlefield.

HANNIBAL

> Stop in the city of Hannibal to learn more about famous author Mark Twain. Twain wrote *The Adventures of Tom Sawyer* and *Adventures of Huckleberry Finn*. His real name was Samuel Clemens. Clemens grew up in Hannibal, and many buildings there are named after him.

Start your day at the Mark Twain Boyhood Home and Museum. The museum's Interpretive Center has exhibits and stories of Twain's childhood. You'll learn which people and places from his life he later used in his writing. Then make your way to Twain's small house. His family moved here when he was nine years old. Twain used his childhood adventures as inspiration for *Tom Sawyer*.

Later, head to the nearby Mark Twain Cave Complex. Twain wrote about the cave in five different books. Take a tour and explore the tall, narrow tunnels. You can even watch a live show with an actor playing Twain. You'll learn about life during the 1800s.

CAVE FORMATION

The inside of the Mark Twain Cave is made of soft Louisiana limestone. However, the entrance is man-made. The cave is more than one hundred million years old. Water leaked into cracks in the limestone, creating tunnels. The tunnels and rooms of the cave formed slowly. Unlike most other caves, the Mark Twain Cave does not have many rock formations inside. Instead, it has narrow tunnels.

The town pharmacy is one of the buildings you can visit in Hannibal.

MERAMEC CAVERNS

> Missouri is often called the Cave State. It has more than six thousand caves, including caverns, to explore! Take a tour of the Meramec Caverns in Stanton. This is one of the largest caves the public can visit in Missouri.

Sign up for a 1.25-mile-long (2 km) guided tour. Trained rangers will lead your group through lit walkways and tunnels. Listen as they tell about the cave's history and point out rock formations. Be sure to look up. The cavern is taller than a seven-story building! During the month of June, the cave offers Lantern Tours. Carry a lantern through the cave. You'll meet actors dressed as historical people such as an American Indian and a soldier along the way.

During the summer months, visitors can buy bags of dirt and use them to pan for gold, fossils, and gems. You may take home your findings! Before you leave the caverns, stop at Granny's Candy Store for some homemade fudge and other sweets.

You'll see cool rock formations throughout the Meramec Caverns.

What treasures will you find in your bag of dirt from Meramec Caverns?

See King Kong outside the Hollywood Wax Museum.

BRANSON

> Travel to Branson for a variety of fun activities. This city is a popular destination with live shows, entertaining museums, and amusement parks.

The Ripley's Believe It or Not! Odditorium in Branson was built to look as if it was split apart by an earthquake. There are more than 450 exhibits to see. You'll find sculptures made out of car parts and scrap metal. Play games and see weird illusions.

Branson has many other fun places to visit too. Check out the Hollywood Wax Museum. See wax figures of all of your favorite movie stars and singers. See Mount Rushmore with new faces. Or look for the cast of *The Wizard of Oz*. You'll learn new things about each person as you walk through the museum. Don't forget to take your picture with your favorite celebrities!

Look for wax versions of celebrities, such as Johnny Depp, at the Hollywood Wax Museum.

THE LAKE OF THE OZARKS

> Enjoy the outdoors at the Lake of the Ozarks in central Missouri. You can set up camp at one of the state parks. The Ha Ha Tonka State Park is perfect for the adventurer. Scale a big hill and visit the remains of a stone castle built in the 1900s. Here you'll enjoy a fantastic view of the lake and surrounding areas. Spend a day on the water. You can swim, boat, or fish.

Next, head to Timber Falls Indoor Waterpark for water fun. A giant bucket tips every minute. It dumps more than 600 gallons (2,272 liters) of water on the people below. That's about two hot tubs full! Try one of the park's waterslides. Or enjoy a relaxing trip on the lazy river.

See the ruins of a castle built by a wealthy businessman in Ha Ha Tonka State Park.

BAGNELL DAM

Bagnell Dam was built between 1929 and 1931 to create electricity for Saint Louis. This concrete wall cuts across the Osage River. When the dam was built, the Osage River flooded nearby farmland. That created the Lake of the Ozarks. The lake has more than 1,300 miles (2,100 km) of shoreline.

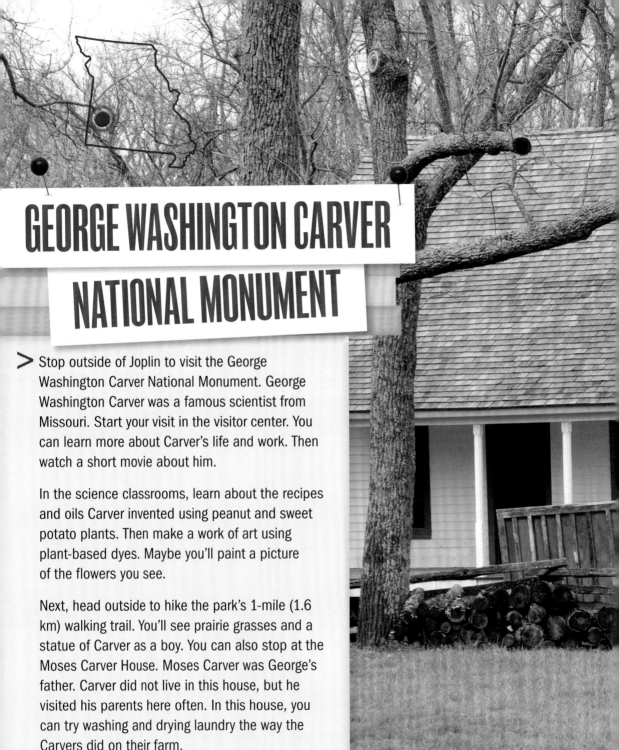

GEORGE WASHINGTON CARVER

NATIONAL MONUMENT

> Stop outside of Joplin to visit the George Washington Carver National Monument. George Washington Carver was a famous scientist from Missouri. Start your visit in the visitor center. You can learn more about Carver's life and work. Then watch a short movie about him.

In the science classrooms, learn about the recipes and oils Carver invented using peanut and sweet potato plants. Then make a work of art using plant-based dyes. Maybe you'll paint a picture of the flowers you see.

Next, head outside to hike the park's 1-mile (1.6 km) walking trail. You'll see prairie grasses and a statue of Carver as a boy. You can also stop at the Moses Carver House. Moses Carver was George's father. Carver did not live in this house, but he visited his parents here often. In this house, you can try washing and drying laundry the way the Carvers did on their farm.

GEORGE WASHINGTON CARVER

George Washington Carver was a scientist and inventor. He was born in southern Missouri in the mid-1800s. He was one of the most successful African American scientists of his time. Carver's most important discoveries were made in farming. He worked with peanut plants and sweet potatoes to help farmers have more successful harvests. He tested soil qualities and created recipes using these crops.

Look at the birds and the plants around you at George Washington Carver National Monument.

Which barbecue food will be your favorite after taking one of the KC Barbecue Tours?

KANSAS CITY BARBECUE

> Hungry? Missouri has some great food! A favorite food is Kansas City barbecue. The delicious dish is made with pork, chicken, or beef that is slow-cooked and smoked in a pit. Missourians have been making barbecue this way since the early 1900s. These days, Kansas City has more than one hundred barbecue restaurants.

Taste a yummy bit of history when you stop by Gates Bar-B-Q in Kansas City. This restaurant has been open since 1946. The tasty barbecue sauce is famous. Try a sandwich, ribs, beans, or fries during your visit to one of Gates's six locations.

If you can't pick just one restaurant to visit, sign up for one of the KC Barbecue Tours. Hop on a bus and listen as your guide gives you a barbecue history lesson. You'll stop at several restaurants along the way. See how chefs prepare and smoke the meat. Taste a sample at each stop. Which is your favorite? You'll leave this tour full of tasty food!

Try Missouri's famous barbecued ribs during your visit.

YOUR TOP TEN

There are lots of things to see and places to visit in the Show-Me State! Did you pick out any favorites? Think about where you would like to go in Missouri. Write down your own top ten list. When you've made your choices, search the Internet or magazines for photos or illustrations—or draw your own. Use the pictures to create a book just like this one.

MISSOURI BY MAP

> MAP KEY

⬢ Capital city

◯ City

◯ Point of interest

▲ Highest elevation

–·– State border

Visit www.lerneresource.com to learn more about the state flag of Missouri.

Missouri River

NEBRASKA

KANSAS

Saint Joseph

KC Barbecue Tours
Gates Bar-B-Q

Kansas City

Independence

Blue Springs

Lee's Summit

Bagnell Dam

Lake of the Ozarks

Timber Falls Indoor Waterpark

Ha Ha Tonka State Park

Wilson's Creek National Battlefield

George Washington Carver National Monument (Diamond)

Springfield

OZARK PLATEAU

OKLAHOMA

Branson

Ripley's Believe It or Not! Odditorium

Hollywood Wax Museum

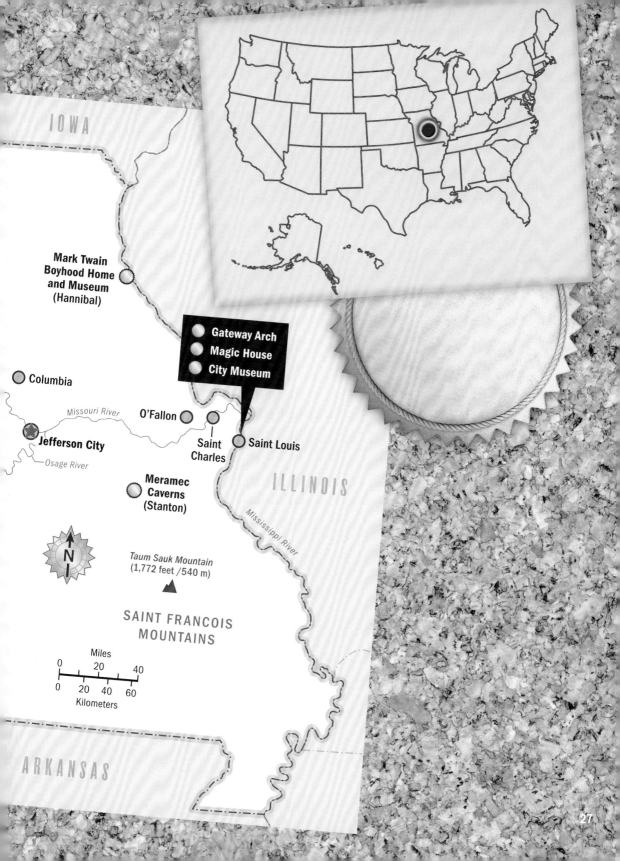

IOWA

Mark Twain
Boyhood Home
and Museum
(Hannibal)

Gateway Arch
Magic House
City Museum

Columbia

Missouri River

O'Fallon

Jefferson City

Saint
Charles

Saint Louis

Osage River

ILLINOIS

Meramec
Caverns
(Stanton)

Mississippi River

N

Taum Sauk Mountain
(1,772 feet /540 m)

SAINT FRANCOIS
MOUNTAINS

Miles
0   20   40
0   20   40   60
Kilometers

ARKANSAS

MISSOURI FACTS

NICKNAME: The Show-Me State

SONG: "Missouri Waltz," by James Royce Shannon and John Valentine Eppel

MOTTO: *Salus Populi Suprema Lex Esto*, or "The Welfare of the People Shall Be the Supreme Law"

> **FLOWER:** hawthorn

TREE: flowering dogwood

> **BIRD:** eastern bluebird

ANIMALS: Missouri mule, honeybee

FOOD: ice-cream cone

DATE AND RANK OF STATEHOOD: August 10, 1821; the 24th state

> **CAPITAL:** Jefferson City

AREA: 69,703 square miles (180,530 sq. km)

AVERAGE JANUARY TEMPERATURE: 30°F (−1°C)

AVERAGE JULY TEMPERATURE: 78°F (26°C)

POPULATION AND RANK: 6,044,171; 18th (2013)

MAJOR CITIES AND POPULATIONS: Kansas City (467,007), Saint Louis (318,416), Springfield (164,122), Independence (117,240), Columbia (115,276)

NUMBER OF US CONGRESS MEMBERS: 8 representatives, 2 senators

NUMBER OF ELECTORAL VOTES: 10

NATURAL RESOURCES: coal, lead, lime, limestone, portland cement

> **AGRICULTURAL PRODUCTS:** corn, cotton, hay, hogs, milk, rice, turkeys, wheat

MANUFACTURED GOODS: chemicals, metal products, machinery, transportation equipment

STATE HOLIDAYS AND CELEBRATIONS: Fair Saint Louis

GLOSSARY

detective: a person whose job it is to find information about something or someone

exhibit: an object or a collection of objects that are on display

harvest: the gathering of ripe crops

illusion: something that looks different from what it is

monument: a building or a statue that honors a person or an event

reenactment: a restaging of a historical event

Union: the Northern states during the Civil War

LERNER

SOURCE

Expand learning beyond the printed book. Download free, complementary educational resources for this book from our website, www.lerneresource.com.

FURTHER INFORMATION

George Washington Carver National Monument: Activity Book
http://www.nps.gov/gwca/planyourvisit/upload/Jr-Ranger-Book-The-Plant
-Doctor-SEP2011.pdf
Print this booklet before visiting the George Washington Carver National
Monument. You can even do some of the activities before your visit!

Gould, Jane. *George Washington Carver*. New York: PowerKids, 2013. Learn
more about this famous scientist and inventor from Missouri.

Jordan, Shirley. *Benjamin Brown and the Great Steamboat Race.* Minneapolis:
Millbrook Press, 2011. This book tells the story of the 1870 steamboat race
from New Orleans to Saint Louis.

Marsico, Katie. *The Missouri River*. North Mankato, MN: Cherry Lake, 2013.
Find out about the history, the wildlife, and the importance of the Missouri
River.

Missouri Secretary of State Kids Page
http://www.sos.mo.gov/kids
This site is filled with games and facts about the Show-Me State.

Missouri Timeline of History
http://www.sos.mo.gov/archives/history/timeline/timeline1.asp#detail
Explore this timeline to learn more about Missouri's history year by year.

INDEX

PHOTO ACKNOWLEDGMENTS

The images in this book are used with the permission of: © American Spirit/Shutterstock Images, pp. 1, 4; NASA, pp. 2–3; © Laura Westlund/Independent Picture Service, pp. 5 (top), 27; © Davel5957/iStockphoto, p. 5 (bottom); © clearviewstock/Shutterstock Images, pp. 6–7; © Bill Greenblatt/UPI/Newscom, pp. 7 (bottom); © Dale Morrow/iStock/Thinkstock, p. 7 (top); © H. Michael Miley CC 2.0, pp. 8–9; © Steve Moses CC 2.0, pp. 9, 21 (bottom); © Jay Goebel/Alamy, pp. 10–11; © The Magic House, pp. 10, 11; © Brandon Alms/Shutterstock Images, pp. 12–13; © Jo Naylor CC 2.0, p. 13; © Tom Uhlenbrock/MCT/Newscom, pp. 14–15, 21 (top); © Larry Jacobsen CC 2.0, p. 15 (bottom); © Buddy Mays/Alamy, p. 15 (top); © Todd Nappen CC 2.0, pp. 16–17; © Jinx! CC 2.0, p. 17 (bottom); © Andrew Warren CC 2.0, p. 17 (top); © Andre Jenny Stock Connection Worldwide/Newscom, pp. 18–19; © Terrance Klassen/Age Fotostock/Alamy, p. 18; © Cliff CC 2.0, p. 19; © Dakota Callaway CC 2.0, pp. 20–21; Courtesy of the Missouri Division of Tourism, pp. 22–23; Public Domain, p. 23 (top); National Park Service, p. 23 (bottom); © Todd Feeback/The Kansas City Star/AP Images, pp. 24–25; © Stuart Monk/Shutterstock Images, p. 24; © Orlin Wagner/AP Images, p. 25; © nicoolay/iStockphoto, p. 26; © Mantonature/iStockphoto, p. 29 (top); © Steve Byland/iStockphoto, p. 29 (middle left); Jack E. Boucher/Library of Congress, p. 29 (middle right) (HABS MO,26-JEFCI,10—15); © Alejandro Rivera/iStockphoto, p. 29 (bottom).

Front cover: © iStockphoto.com/pawel.gaul (St. Louis); David R. Frazier/DanitaDelimont.com "Danita Delimont Photography"/Newscom (Riverboat); © SuperStock (Sculpture); © Laura Westlund/Independent Picture Service (map); © iStockphoto.com/fpm (seal); © iStockphoto.com/vicm (pushpins); © iStockphoto.com/benz190 (corkboard).